DATE DUE

DISCARD

DEMCO 38-296

Apple
Creatures
Make Your Own

Iryna Stepanova

Sergiy Kabachenko

FIREFLY BOOKS

Contents

Introduction

The apple. It is one of our most ancient and popular fruits. Its nutritional value has long been known. "An apple a day keeps the doctor away," goes the popular saying. The apple, however, stands for more than just good health. It is also a symbol of youth, beauty, spring and marriage. It has become a powerful symbol in many myths, legends and fairytales.

Paris, the mythical hero of Greek legend, in order to settle a disagreement between three goddesses (Here, Aphrodite and Athena), was made to present to one of them a golden apple as a mark of that goddess' superior beauty. He awarded the apple to Aphrodite, who had promised him the most beautiful mortal woman in the world—Helen of Troy, wife of the Spartan King, Menelaus. This in turn sparked the great Trojan War, and the European saying, "An apple is a sign of strife."

The color and leaves of the apple historically played an important role in many ancient wedding rites, where if a young girl accepted an apple from a suitor, she was effectively agreeing to marry him. The apple was also used as a wedding invitation.

In today's busy world, apples can turn any day into a holiday, and easily settle the age-old question of "What's for dessert?" Children love apples and other fruits, especially when worked into charming and fantastical shapes and figures.

The most important thing to remember when working with cut apples is to sprinkle them with lemon juice immediately after cutting in order to prevent browning. As for the rest—it's all in your hands!

Dog 1

INGREDIENTS

2 yellow apples
1 red grape
1 blue grape
7 green grapes

1 Place the apple upside down and cut off a piece at a downward angle.

2 Place the piece of apple with the cut side down and cut off a thin slice from the top.

3 Cut the slice into two pieces. This is the muzzle. Place the two parts of the muzzle on the cut surface of the apple as shown. This is the mouth.

4 Cut off a thin slice from the red grape for the tongue.

5 Insert the tongue into the mouth.

6 Cut off a small round slice from the blue grape. This is the nose.

7 Place the nose on the muzzle.

8 Cut off two circles from a green grape.

9 These are the eyes.

10 Cut off two tiny circles from the blue grape for the pupils. Lay them on the eyes.

11 Cut off a thin slice from the remaining apple piece.

12 Cut this slice in half. These are the ears. Place them on the head.

13 Place the second whole apple next to the head. This is the body. Lay four grapes under the body as the legs.

14 Slice two green grapes in half. Place one grape half against each leg. These are the paws.

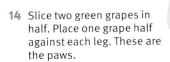

Chicken

INGREDIENTS

1 yellow apple
1 slice of red apple
2 red grapes
1 blue grape

1 Place the apple upside down. Cut a piece of it at an angle.

2 Place the piece of apple with the cut downwards and cut off a thin slice from it.

3 Cut a slice in two parts. The bigger piece is the head, the smaller is the crest.

4 Remaining apple (step 1) is the body.

5 Place the head on the body.

6 Place the crest behind the head.

7 Cut off two small tiny circles from blue grapes. These are ears.

8 Cut a thin slice of red apple for the beak.

9 Place the eyes and beak on the head.

10 Cut off thin slice from the remaining apple.

11 Cut the slice in two. These are wings.

12 Put them on the body.

13 Slice a red grape in two. These are the feet.

Clown

INGREDIENTS

2 red apples
1 yellow apple
2 red grapes
1 blue grape
1 blueberry
1 raspberry

1 Cut a round slice from the bottom of the yellow apple.

2 Cut out a small segment near the top of the apple.

3 Cut the same sized segment from the red apple and then a smaller segment from that. This is the mouth.

4 Cut out about one quarter of the apple as shown. Insert the lips.

5 With the apple upside down, make a round hole for the nose.

8

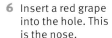

6 Insert a red grape into the hole. This is the nose.

7 Cut a thin slice from the larger rear apple section that was cut off (step 4).

8 Cut this slice into two halves to make ears. Place them as shown.

9 Secure the ears with the cut section.

10 Cut a circle from a red grape. Cut it in half. These are the eyes.

11 Cut the blueberry in half and place one half on each eye. These are the pupils.

12 Make vertical incisions around the round slice (step 1). This is the hair. Place it on the head.

13 Cut a slice off the bottom of the red apple. This is the hat.

14 Place the hat on the head. Put a raspberry on top as a pompon.

15 Place the red apple on its cut base. This is the body. Put the head on top.

16 For boots, cut the blue grape in half and place below the body. Cut two matchstick arms from the red apples.

Bear

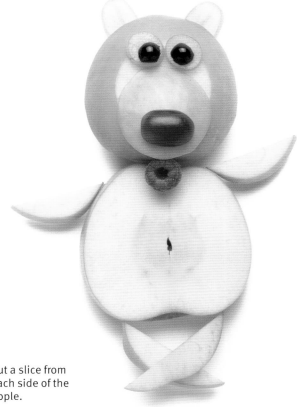

INGREDIENTS

1 green apple
2 green grapes
1 red grape
1 blueberry
1 raspberry

1 Cut a slice from each side of the apple.

2 Cut two thin slices from the middle piece of the apple.

3 Lay one of the side slices skin side down. This is the back of the head.

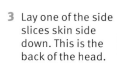

4 For the ears, cut a green grape lengthwise into four slices. The middle slices are the ears.

5 Place the ears on the back of the head.

6 The other slice of the apple (step 1) is the front of the head. Cut a small circle from the top. This is the muzzle.

7 Put the front of the head on the back.

8 For the eyes, slice two circles from a green grape.

9 For pupils, cut the blueberry in half and place on the eyes.

10 Lay the muzzle on the head. Use half of a red grape as a nose.

12 For arms and legs, cut out four small segments from the second slice of apple (step 2).

11 For the body, lay the center slice (step 1) below the head. Use a raspberry as the mouth.

13 Place the legs on the body.

Moose

INGREDIENTS

1 red apple
1 green grape
1 blue grape
1 blueberry

1 Cut the red apple in half lengthwise.

2 Take one apple half and cut a small circle from the skin side. The remaining half is the body.

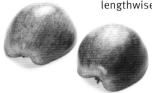

3 Cut two side slices from the other half. These are the legs.

4 Cut two more slices from the center piece of apple.

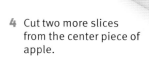

5 The side slices are antlers. The middle part is the muzzle.

6 Make teeth-like incisions in the antlers.

7 Place the muzzle and horns on the body (step 2).

8 Cut two side slices off the small circle (step 2). These are ears.

9 Place the ears beside the muzzle.

10 To make eyes, cut two circles from the green grape.

11 Cut the blueberry in half for the pupils.

12 Put the legs (step 3) against the body.

13 Cut the blue grape into halves. These are the hooves.

14 Put the hooves below the legs.

15 You can also make legs from matchstick pieces of apple.

Bunny

INGREDIENTS

1 yellow apple
2 red grapes
1 blue grape
4 green grapes

1. With the apple upside down, cut a piece across the top center at an angle.

2. Place the remaining piece of apple skin side up and cut off a round slice from the top.

3. Cut another thin slice from the apple piece.

4. To make ears, cut this slice in half. Place them on the first slice (step 2). This is the head.

5. Cut the round slice (step 2) into two pieces. Place the smaller piece on top of the ears. This is the muzzle.

6 For the teeth, cut a thin slice from a red grape. Cut the slice in half. Place the teeth below the muzzle.

7 For the cheeks, cut a green grape in half lengthwise. Place under the muzzle.

8 For the nose, cut off a tip from the blue grape.

9 Lay it on the muzzle.

10 For the eyes, slice two circles from a red grape.

11 Place the circles on the muzzle.

12 For pupils, cut two tips from a blue grape. Place them on the eyes.

13 Cut three green grapes into halves. Use four halves for the back legs.

14 Use the remaining two halves for the front feet.

Pig

INGREDIENTS

1 red apple, with stem
apple seeds
2 red grapes
1 green grape
1 blueberry

1 Cut a side slice from the red apple. This is the muzzle. Cut two more thin slices. The medium slice is the head, the large is the body.

2 Cut the red grape in half lengthwise.

3 For the ears, cut one of the halves in half lengthwise.

4 Cut a thin circle from the other red grape. This is the mouth.

5 Place the muzzle (step 1) on the head.

6 Cut two circles from the green grape. These are eyes. Place above the muzzle.

7 Use apple seeds for the pupils.

8 Use two red grape circles (step 4) for the nostrils.

9 Put the nostrils on the muzzle. Lay the body (step 1) next to the head.

10 Cut out legs from an apple slice.

11 Cut the blueberry in half. These are hooves.

12 Place the hooves below the legs. Use the apple stem for the tail.

Cat

INGREDIENTS

1 red apple
1 blueberry
1 green grape
2 red grapes
pomegranate seeds

1 Cut the apple in half. One half is the body.

2 From the other half, cut out two small slots as shown. These are the cheeks.

3 From the same half, cut two edge slices of equal size. These are the ears.

4 Cut one more side slice for the tail. The remaining piece is the head.

5 Insert the ears into the slots. Place the cheeks against the head.

6 Cut the tip and one round slice from a red grape. The tip is the nose, the circle is the mouth.

7 Place the mouth between the cheeks. Place the nose over the mouth.

9 Place the eyes above the nose.

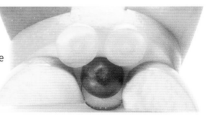

8 Cut two round slices from the green grape. These are the eyes.

10 Cut the blueberry in half. These are the pupils.

11 Put the head on the body.

12 Cut a red grape in half lengthwise and place against the body as legs. Lay out pomegranate seeds as toes.

13 You can also make a different pose.

Sheep

INGREDIENTS

1 green apple
1 green grape
1 red grape
2 blueberries
red currant stems,
    with berries

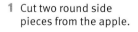

1 Cut two round side pieces from the apple.

2 Cut a small round slice from one of them. The round slice is a muzzle.

3 Cut a thin slice from the middle part of the apple.

4 Lay the middle part flat. Place the small slice (step 2) on top, cut side up. This is the head.

5 Place the muzzle (step 2) on the head.

6 For the eyes, cut two round slices from a green grape.

7 For the pupils, cut one blueberry in half.

8 From a slice of green grape, cut off two side pieces.

9 Place these on the muzzle as the nose.

10 Cut the red grape in half lengthwise.

11 Cut one of the halves in two. These are the mouth.

12 Arrange the red currant stems around the head.

13 Cut small segments from an apple slice. Two of these are ears.

14 Place the ears on either side of the head among the red currant stems. Cut out strips of the apple are for the legs. Cut the other blueberry into quarters. Place one quarter against each leg. These are the hooves.

Lion

INGREDIENTS

1 red apple
1 green grape
2 blue grapes
1 red grape
1 blueberry

1 Cut the apple in and cut off a round slice. This is the body.

2 Put the half with the smaller cut side down. This is the mane.

3 From the other half, cut two slices from each side. The middle part is the muzzle.

4 Place the muzzle on the mane.

5 Cut the sides off the thin circle (step 1). The middle piece, cut side up, is the tongue.

6 Place the tongue under the head. Cut the red grape in half for the ears.

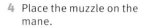

7 Cut the green grape in half. Cut a thin round slice from each half.

8 Cut each half in three as shown.

9 Cut a thin round slice from a blue grape. Cut this slice in half.

10 Insert the blue grape halves between two end slices of green grape. This is an eye.

11 Set each eye onto a thin round slice of green grape.

12 Make one more eye. Place them on the head.

13 Cut a blue grape in half on an oblique angle.

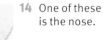

14 One of these is the nose.

15 From the remaining apple slices, lay out the body, legs and tail.

Heron

INGREDIENTS

1 red apple

1 green apple

1 green grape

1 red grape

1 blue grape

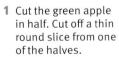

1 Cut the green apple in half. Cut off a thin round slice from one of the halves.

2 Cut one more round slice. The remaining piece is the body.

3 Cut the red apple in half. From one half, cut four side slices.

4 One edge slice is the tail. Place it under the body.

5 Cut out claws from the second edge slice.

6 Cut wings from the other two end slices.

7 Place the wings on the body. Secure with the slice of green apple.

8 Cut a top slice from the middle of the red apple (step 3).

9 Cut off the ends of the remaining piece on an angle. This is the neck.

10 Set the neck on the body.

11 Cut two thin slices from the sides of the top slice. These are the legs.

12 Cut a triangle off the remaining piece. This is the top part of the beak.

13 Carve the remaining piece as shown to make the bottom part of the beak.

14 To make eyes, place two thin, round green grape slices on top of a slice of red grape. Use tiny tips of blue grape for pupils.

15 Place the eyes on the bottom part of the beak.

16 Put the top part of the beak on top. Place the head on the neck.

17 Lay the legs and claws against the body.

Hippo

INGREDIENTS
1 green apple
5 green grapes
1 blue grape

1 Cut the apple in half.

2 Cut a round slice from one of the halves. This is the muzzle.

3 Cut one more slice. This is the head.

4 The remaining half is the body. Place the head on the body.

5 Lay the muzzle on the head.

6 Cut a green grape in half.

7 Cut rounds from each grape half. These are the ears.

8 From each tip of grape, cut a slice on each side.

9 Cut a round from the blue grape. Cut this in half.

10 Insert one blue grape half between the side slices of green grape. This is an eye.

11 Make another eye. Place the eyes on the head. Lay the ears on the head.

12 Use four green grapes for legs.

Lamb

INGREDIENTS

1 yellow apple
apple seeds
3 red grapes
2 leaves of mint

1 Place the apple on its top and cut off a piece at a downward angle.

2 Put the piece of apple with the cut side down and cut a slice off the top.

3 Cut the top in two as shown. This is the head.

4 The remaining apple is the body.

5 Place the head on the body.

6 Put two leaves of mint under the head as ears.

7 For eyes, cut a red grape circle in half.

8 Put the eyes on the head.

9 Use apple seeds as pupils.

10 Cut a tip from a red grape.

11 With cut sides down, cut each tip in two. These are legs.

12 Make four legs and place them below the body.

Owl

INGREDIENTS

1 yellow apple
2 red grapes
2 green grapes
1 blue grape
1 stalk of mint

1 Place the apple on its base. Cut a small round slice off one side as shown. Then cut two more thin round slices.

2 Put one round slice on top of the apple base. This is the head.

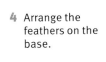

3 To make feathers, slice the green grapes into thin rounds. Cut each round in half.

4 Arrange the feathers on the base.

5 For the wings, cut two side segments from the second apple slice.

6 Cut out "L" eyebrows from the remaining piece.

7 Place the eyebrows on the head.

8 Cut the blue grape into thin slices lengthwise. Use two middle slices for the eyes.

9 Cut two side pieces as shown from one of the end slices. These are pupils. The middle is the beak.

10 Place the pupils on the eyes and the beak as shown.

11 Lay the wings against the body. Use mint stalks for the crest.

12 Cut out claws from the halves of a red grape.

13 Lay these below the body.

Mouse

INGREDIENTS

1 red apple

2 red grapes

1 green grape

1 blueberry

1 Cut off two small edge slices from the apple, and three more thin slices of varying sizes.

2 Put the smallest slice on top of the biggest slice. This is the head.

3 Lay the edge slices against the head. These are ears.

4 Cut the tip of a green grape in half. These are the eyelids.

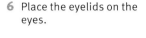

5 Slice two rounds from the remainder of the of green grape. These are the eyes.

6 Place the eyelids on the eyes.

7 Cut the blueberry in half. Cut one half in two. These are the pupils.

8 Place the pupils on the eyes as shown.

9 Cut the red grape in half lengthwise. Use one half as the muzzle.

10 For the nose, cut the blueberry in half and place one half on the head. This is the muzzle. Lay the apple slice next to the head. This is the body.

11 Cut the second red grape into quarters lengthwise.

12 Use one quarter of the red grape as the front leg and the remaining half as the back leg.

13 Use two more of the quarters for the paws. Cut a thin strip of apple for the tail.

Wolf

INGREDIENTS

2 yellow apples
1 green grape
2 blue grapes
1 blueberry

1 Place the apple on its top. Cut off a thick slice at an angle. This is the muzzle.

2 Cut off a thin slice from the apple. The remaining apple is the head.

3 Using a small corer or strawberry huller, make two holes in the back of the head for the ears.

4 Make a hole in the lower part of muzzle for the nose.

5 For the ears, cut two segments off the thin apple slice.

6 Insert the ears into the holes in the head. Lay the muzzle against the head.

7 Cut the ends off the green grape. Cut the middle part of the grape into two thick rounds. These are the eyes.

8 Put the eyes on the head above the muzzle.

9 For the pupils, cut two round tips off the blueberry. Place the pupils on the eyes. Insert a blue grape in the hole in the muzzle for the nose.

10 Cut an edge slice at an angle from the second apple. This is the body. Cut off a second thin slice.

11 Cut two narrow segments from the thin apple slice. One segment is the tail.

12 Cut out "L"-shaped legs from the remaining piece.

13 Place the body beside the head, and the legs and tail as shown.

Bull

INGREDIENTS

1 red apple
1 red grape
1 green grape
1 blueberry
2 raspberries

1 Cut the apple in half lengthwise. From one half, cut out two pieces as shown. These are the horns.

2 From the same half, cut an edge slice from each side. These are the ears.

3 Cut one more slice. This will be the lower part of the muzzle.

4 The remaining piece is the head. Insert the horns and ears as shown.

5 Cut two thin rounds from the green grape. These are the eyes.

6 Place the eyes on the head. Cut blueberry halves for the pupils.

7 Cut the red grape in half lengthwise.

8 Cut one half in two again lengthwise. These are eyebrows. Place as shown.

9 Cut a thin round slice from the second apple half. This is the body. The remaining part is the top part of the muzzle.

10 Lay the top part of the muzzle on the bottom part.

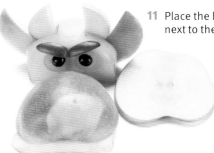

11 Place the body next to the head.

12 Cut thin strips of apple for the legs and tail.

13 Put two raspberries against the legs. These are hooves.

Squirrel

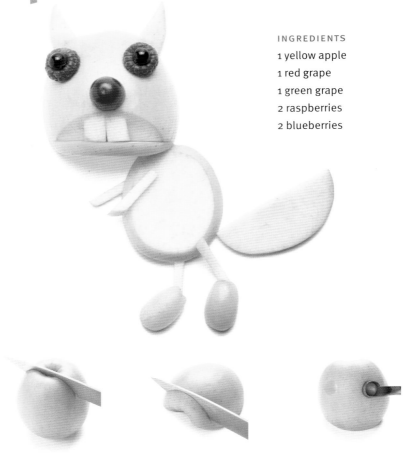

INGREDIENTS

1 yellow apple
1 red grape
1 green grape
2 raspberries
2 blueberries

1 Place the apple on its top. Cut a side slice slightly less than half of the apple.

2 Cut a small slice off the bottom of the slice.

3 Put the slice cut side down. Make two holes for eyes. This is the head.

4 Cut out a "V" segment near the bottom. This is the mouth.

5 Peel the skin off this segment.

6 Cut out two teeth from the middle part of the segment.

7 Insert the teeth into the mouth.

8 Cut the peel in two. These are the ears. Make incisions in the top of the head and insert the ears.

9 Use the raspberries for eyes and the blueberries as pupils.

10 Insert the pupils into the eyes. Insert the eyes into the holes.

11 Use a red grape half for the nose. Lay the nose on the head.

12 Cut a side slice off the remaining apple half. Cut off another thin slice for the body.

13 Cut one more thin round slice. Cut two narrow strips from the center as shown. Use one of the wide side pieces as a tail.

14 Cut each strip in half to use as arms and legs.

15 Cut a green grape in half and use as feet. Place the tail beside the body.

Dog 2

INGREDIENTS

1 green apple
1 slice of a red apple
5 green grapes

1 blue grape
1 blueberry

1 Cut two side pieces from the apple.

2 Cut a small round slice from the top of one half. The rest is the muzzle.

3 Cut one more slice from the middle part of the apple. Lay the small round on this slice, cut side up. This is the head.

4 Lay the muzzle on top of the head.

5 Cut a green grape in half. Cut a thin slice from one half. This is one eye.

6 Place the eye on the head. Use half of the blueberry as a pupil.

7 Cut two side segments from the other grape half. This is the second eye.

8 Cut a small round from the blue grape. Cut the round in half.

9 Place this slice of blue grape between the green grape segments. This is the second eye, winking.

10 Cut a slice from the remaining apple. Cut four segments as shown.

11 Place two segments on the head as the ears.

12 Cut two segments out of the red apple slice. Cut teeth out of one of them.

13 Insert the two red segments into the muzzle to make the mouth. Use half of the blue grape for the nose.

14 Use the second side slice (step 1) as the body. Cut out four thin apple strips for the legs. Use grapes for paws.

15 Use a small segment of apple for the tail.

Rabbit

INGREDIENTS

1 green apple
3 slices of red apple   1 red grape
2 green grapes   1 blueberry

1 Cut the green apple in half.

2 Cut a thin, small round from one half.

3 Cut the small round slice into two parts, one slightly larger than the other. These make the muzzle.

4 Cut one more round slice. This is the head.

5 The remaining part of the apple half is the body.

6 Place a green grape against the body. This is the tail.

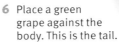

7 Cut the three slices of red apple in half.

8 Cut two segments and two triangles from each half as shown. These are the ears and legs.

9 Place the legs and ears against the body.

10 Place the head on the body.

11 Place the muzzle on the head.

12 For eyes, cut two rounds from a green grape. For pupils, cut the blueberry in half. Place the eyes on the head.

13 Use one half of the red grape for the nose.

Fish

INGREDIENTS
1 green apple
2 red grapes
1 blue grape
1 blueberry

1 Cut two side slices from an apple.

2 Cut a thin round slice from the middle part. The remainder is the body. Cut out two segments for the fins, one bigger, for the tail.

3 Lay one side slice cut side up. Place the tail and fins on top, as shown.

4 Cut a red grape in half lengthwise.

5 Place one half on the edge of the body.

6 Cut the second half lengthwise again.

7 Place one quarter against the half. This is the mouth.

8 Place the second side slice of apple on top.

9 Cut a thin round from the blue grape. This is an eye.

10 Place the eye on the fish.

11 Cut the blueberry in half.

12 Put one half on the eye. This is the pupil.

13 Make another eye. Place it between the apple slices.

Boxer

INGREDIENTS

1 red apple
3 green grapes
1 blue grape
1 blueberry
2 raspberries
mint leaves

1 Cut off the bottom of the apple. Set aside. Cut off a slice ½ in. thick.

2 Place the slice cut side down. Make an incision in the form of a semicircle and slice the peel off the contours.

3 Make incisions in the apple pulp for the teeth.

4 Cut two thin round slices from the bottom of the apple. Remove any seeds.

5 Cut one slice into three parts.

6 In one end of the center piece, make teeth-like incisions. This is the hair.

7 Cut one of the side pieces in half. Round off the wide edge of each. These are the ears.

8 Place the top part of the apple, skin side down. This is the head.

9 Place the ears and hair on the head. Cover with the slice with teeth.

10 Place the bottom (step 1) on top. This is the face.

11 Lay a whole green grape on the face for the nose. Cut two thin rounds from a green grape for the eyes. Cut a thin round from the blue grape and place under one eye for the bruise. Make pupils from blueberry halves.

12 Cut the second slice of apple into strips as shown.

13 Use these for the body, legs and arms, as shown.

14 Use the raspberries as boxing gloves, a green grape cut in half as boots, and the mint leaves as shorts.

15 You can also transform the boxer into a king.

Spider

INGREDIENTS

1 green apple
1 red grape
1 blueberry

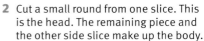

1 Cut side slices from the apple.

2 Cut a small round from one slice. This is the head. The remaining piece and the other side slice make up the body.

3 Cut a thin round slice from the middle part of the apple.

4 Cut the slice into 8 strips. These are the legs. Use the two side segments as supports for the eyes.

5 Put the eye supports on the bottom part of the body.

6 Put the head on top of the eye supports.

7 Arrange the legs around the body.

8 Cover with the second side slice.

9 Cut two thin rounds from the red grape. Place them on the supports. These are the eyes.

10 Cut a blueberry in half. These are the pupils.

11 Place the pupils on the eyes.

Cat

INGREDIENTS

1 red apple plus
½ red apple
½ green apple
2 green grapes
2 red grapes
1 blueberry

1 Cut the halves of green and red apples into thin bars of identical width.

2 Lay out the body in red and green bars to make stripes.

3 Cut the top off the whole red apple.

4 Then cut off a slice ½ in thick.

5 With the larger side down, cut and peel a semicircle of skin as shown.

6 Make teeth-like incisions in the exposed apple.

7 Cut a thin slice from the remaining apple. Remove the seeds. Cut off a segment.

8 Cut this segment in half. These are the ears.

9 The bottom part of the apple is the head.

10 Place the cut side up and lay the ears on top.

11 Cover this with the slice with the teeth.

12 Place the apple base on top. This is the head.

13 Lay a green grape on top for a nose.

15 Lay the body against the head. Use the remaining apple strips as legs. Attach the tail and place two red grapes as paws.

14 Make eyes from green grape rounds. Use the blueberry, cut in half, for the pupils.

Hedgehog

INGREDIENTS
1 green apple
2 red grapes
1 blueberry

1 Cut two side slices from the apple.

2 Cut off a small round from one side slice. The remaining slice is the bottom part of the body.

3 Cut two thin round slices from the middle part of the apple.

4 Cut one slice into 8 strips. These are the needles.

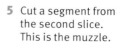

5 Cut a segment from the second slice. This is the muzzle.

6 Place the bottom part of the body skin side down. Arrange the needles on top.

7 Cover with the second side slice. This is the top part of the body.

8 Insert the muzzle between the bottom and top of the body.

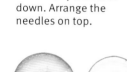

9 Cut two thin rounds from a red grape for the eyes.

10 Cut the blueberry in half for the pupils.

11 Place the pupils on the eyes. Insert one of the eyes between the top and bottom of the body, beside the muzzle. Lay the other eye on top of the body.

12 Cut a red grape in half lengthwise.

13 Use one half for the nose and place on the muzzle.

Dog 3

INGREDIENTS

2 small red apples
2 slices of large red apple
1 blue grape
1 green grape
4 red grapes
1 blueberry

1 Cut a small slice off the small red apple, including the dimple. This is the muzzle. The rest of the apple is the head.

2 For the ears, partially separate a big red apple slice in three pieces. Do not sever the pieces.

3 The center piece (step 2) is the muzzle. Place it on top of the head, let the ears hang. Lay the muzzle on top.

4 Cut the tip off of the green grape.

5 Cut this in half. These are the eyelids.

6 Cut two thin rounds of green grape. These are the eyes.

7 Cut the blueberry in half. Cut one half in half again. These are the pupils.

8 Place the pupils on the eyes. Place the eyelids above the pupils.

9 Place the eyes on the head.

10 For the nose, cut a blue grape in half lengthwise.

11 Place one half on the muzzle.

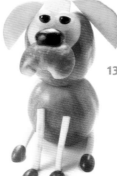

13 Cut apple strips for the legs and the tail, and use grape halves for the paws.

12 Place the second apple against the head. This is the body.

Frog

INGREDIENTS

1 green apple
5 green grapes
1 blueberry

1 Cut the apple in half lengthwise.

2 Cut a thin small round from one half.

3 Cut another thin round slice.

4 The remaining part of this half is the body. Arrange the two slices on the body as shown. This is the head.

5 Cut two thin rounds from the green grape. These are the eyes.

6 Cut the blueberry in half. These are the pupils.

7 Lay the eyes and pupils on the head.

8 Cut a green grape in half lengthwise.

9 Cut feet from each half.

10 Place the feet on the front of the body.

11 For the legs, cut a green grape in half at an angle.

12 Place the legs at the bottom of the body as shown.

Pirate

INGREDIENTS

1 red apple plus
½ r ed apple
½ green apple
2 green grapes
2 red grapes
1 ground cherry
1 blueberry
4 blue grapes

1 Cut off the bottom of the red apple. Set aside. Cut off a slice ½ in. thick.

2 Place the slice cut side down. Make an incision on one side in the form of a semicircle. Slice the peel off the contour.

3 Make incisions in the revealed apple for the teeth.

4 Cut two more thin round slices from the apple. Remove the seeds. Cut two segments from one of the slices.

5 Make incisions in one end of the middle slice. This is the beard.

6 Cut one end segment in half. Round off the wide edges of each. These are the ears.

7 The top part of the apple is the back of the head. Place it skin side down and put the second apple slice on top.

8 Place the ears and beard on the head. Cover them with the slice with the teeth.

9 Place the top of the apple on top, cut side down. This is the face.

10 Cut a small thin round from a green grape for an eye. Cut the tip off a blueberry for one pupil. Lay it on the grape. Use the ground cherry for the nose.

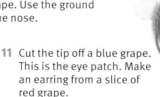

11 Cut the tip off a blue grape. This is the eye patch. Make an earring from a slice of red grape.

12 Cut a round side slice from a green apple. Make parallel incisions across the skin and cut out alternating strips of peel to create stripes. This is the body.

13 Place the body below the head. Make legs from blue grapes and a foot from one red grape. Arms, hands and a wooden leg from slices of apple, as shown.

14 Create a dagger from apple slices.

Crocodile

INGREDIENTS

1 green apple
1 green grape
1 blueberry

1 Cut a thin slice off the bottom of the apple.

2 Cut the slice into four parts. These are the legs.

3 Place the apple cut side down. Cut a slice from the top at an oblique angle. This is the nose.

4 Cut off the top part of the apple. This is the head.

5 Cut the bottom part of the apple into thin round slices.

6 Cut the biggest slice into three pieces.

7 Cut a segment from the smallest slice of apple. This is the tip of the tail. Lay out the slices in the form of a body.

8 Place the head on the body.

9 Put the two segments cut from the biggest slice onto the head.

10 Cut the tip off the green grape. Cut this in half. These are the eyelids.

11 Cut two small thin rounds from the remaining part of the green grape. These are the eyes.

12 Cut a blueberry into quarters. Two of these are the pupils.

13 Place the eyelids on the eyes. Place the pupils against the eyelids.

14 Put the eyes on the head. Make incisions in the middle part of the biggest slice (step 6). Place this piece on the head. This is the muzzle.

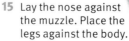

15 Lay the nose against the muzzle. Place the legs against the body.

Hamster

INGREDIENTS

2 green apples
1 red apple
1 green grape
1 red grape
1 blueberry

1 Cut a small slice from the top part of a green apple at an oblique angle with part of the dimple. This is the muzzle.

2 Cut the bottom off the apple. Cut two round thin slices from the apple.

3 The larger of the slices will serve as the base. The remaining part of the apple is the head.

4 Cut out two small rounds from the red apple. These are the ears. Place them on the base.

5 Place the head on top.

6 Cut two segments from the smaller round apple slice.

7 Place these on the head for ears.

8 Cut two thin rounds from the green grape. These are the eyes.

9 Cut the blueberry in half. These are the pupils.

10 Place the pupils on the eyes and put the eyes on the head.

11 Place the muzzle on the head. Use a red grape for the nose.

12 Put a red apple slice against the head.

13 Put the half of the red apple on top of the slice. This is the tummy.

14 Cut two segments from a red apple slice.

15 Cut the segments into two parts as shown.

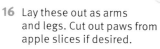

16 Lay these out as arms and legs. Cut out paws from apple slices if desired.

Tyrannosaurus

INGREDIENTS

1 red apple

1 green grape

1 blueberry

1 Cut three thin slices from an apple.

2 Cut one of them into three parts as shown. The biggest piece is the body. The middle triangle is a tail. The small side piece is the neck.

3 Lay out the neck and the tail as shown.

4 Put the body on top.

5 Cut side sections from the second slice. These are legs. The middle part is the head.

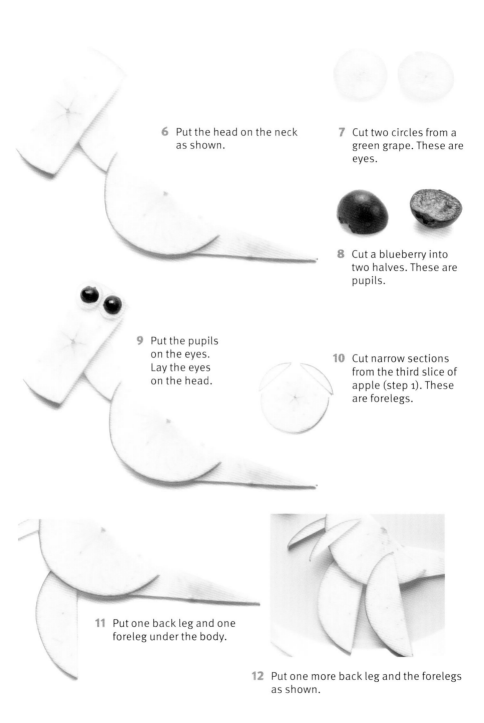

6 Put the head on the neck as shown.

7 Cut two circles from a green grape. These are eyes.

8 Cut a blueberry into two halves. These are pupils.

9 Put the pupils on the eyes. Lay the eyes on the head.

10 Cut narrow sections from the third slice of apple (step 1). These are forelegs.

11 Put one back leg and one foreleg under the body.

12 Put one more back leg and the forelegs as shown.

Stegosaurus

INGREDIENTS

2 slices of green apple

3 slices of red apple

1 red grape

1 blueberry

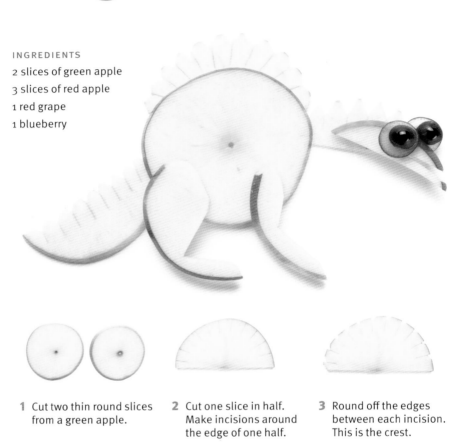

1 Cut two thin round slices from a green apple.

2 Cut one slice in half. Make incisions around the edge of one half.

3 Round off the edges between each incision. This is the crest.

4 On the other half slice, make incisions along the straight edge and round off the edges between the incisions. This is the tail.

66

5 Cut a narrow segment off the second round green slice and cut out teeth along the rounded edge. This is the neck.

6 Cut a similarly-sized narrow segment from a red apple slice. This is the head.

7 Cut out a mouth from one side, as shown.

8 Cut two thin rounds from the red grape. Cut a blueberry in half.

9 Place one grape round on the edge of the neck. Lay a blueberry half on top for the pupil. This is the eye. Cut the second grape round in half and place next to the eye as a base for the head.

10 Place the head on top.

11 Cut one more round from the red grape for the second eye. Place this on the head and add the second pupil.

12 Place the crest next to the neck. Place a round red apple slice over top. This is the body. Insert the tail under the body.

13 Cut one more red apple slice into two slightly unequal parts.

14 Cut out the rear leg from the larger slice, and the front leg from the smaller.

15 Place the legs on the body as shown.

Skipper

INGREDIENTS

1 yellow apple
2 red apples
2 blue grapes
1 green grape
1 blueberry
1 ground cherry

1 Cut off the top and bottom from a red apple.

2 Cut off a piece slightly less than half of the apple. Then cut a thin slice from the middle section.

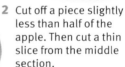

3 Cut the thin slice in half. Carve out arms from the halves.

4 Insert the arms between the apple halves. This is the body.

5 Cut small circles out of another apple slice. These are the buttons.

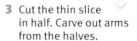

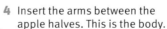

6 Cut a blue grape in half lengthwise to use as boots. Place these below the body.

7 Cut the yellow apple in half crosswise. Slice a thin round from one half.

8 Incise a sunbeam pattern around the slice. This is the beard.

9 Cut a segment off the remainder of the apple half.

10 Make vertical incisions in this piece, for the moustache.

11 Cut a piece out of the remaining part of apple half.

12 Place this piece as shown on the body. This is the head.

13 Cut out a mouth from the other red apple. Place it on the beard with the moustache on top. Cut the green grape in half and attach as the ears.

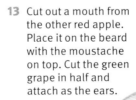

14 Cut the tip off of a blue grape, then cut the tip in half. These are the eyes.

15 Cut out eyelids from a slice of yellow apple.

16 Cut out a nose from the same slice.

17 Cut the top off a red apple. This is the hat. Put the ground cherry on top as a pompom.

Airplane

INGREDIENTS

1 red apple
1 green apple
1 red grape

1 Cut the red apple in half. Cut a thin slice from one half.

2 Cut two side segments from the slice.These are the wings.

3 Cut one more slice. This is the base.

4 Cut a third round slice. Cut this slice on an oblique angle into two parts.

5 Cut the corner off one part. This is the tail.

6 The second half of the apple is the fuselage. Cut a slot for the tail.

7 Cut a small round slice from the front of the fuselage.

8 Place the wings on the base.

9 Place the fuselage on top. Insert the tail.

10 Cut six circles from a red apple slice. These are windows.

11 Lay the windows on the fuselage.

12 Cut a green grape in half. Use one half as the pilots' cabin.

13 Cut a small round slice from a green apple.

14 Cut out a propeller.

15 Lay the propeller on the front of the fuselage. Cut the tip from a red grape and place in the center of the propeller.

Soldier

INGREDIENTS

2 red apples
1 green apple
1 blue grape
1 green grape

1 Cut a red apple in half. Cut a slice from the one half on an oblique angle. The remaining part is the head.

2 Cut the side slice in two parts, as shown.

3 Cut a segment from the oblique slice.

4 Carve teeth around the rounded edge. This is the moustache.

5 Cut a small triangle from the remaining piece.

6 Carve a nose out of it.

7 Place the nose and moustache on the head.

8 Make eyes out of two thin rounds of green grape and two small rounds of blue grape. Place the eyes on the head.

9 Cut the bottom from the green apple. Cut out teeth around it. This is the collar.

10 Cut the top off the whole red apple. The remainder is the body.

11 Place the collar on the body.

12 Place the head on top.

13 Cut an oval slice from the green apple. This is the shield.

14 Lean it against the body.

Ringmaster

INGREDIENTS

2 green apples
1 yellow apple
1 red apple
1 green grape
2 red grapes
1 blueberry
1 ground cherry

1 Cut the yellow apple in half lengthwise. Cut an oblique slice from one half. The remaining part is the head.

2 Cut out a forehead and chin as shown.

3 Cut out a nose from one of the discarded pieces from the forehead.

4 Cut the tip off the green grape and cut it in half again. These are the eyelids. Cut two thin rounds from the green grape for eyes. Cut the blueberry into quarters for the pupils.

5 Place the eyelids on the eyes and lay the pupils under the eyelids.

6 Cut a mouth out of red apple peel.

7 Cut the top and bottom off a green apple. This is the body. Make incisions for the arms.

8 Cut the top in half. These are the arms. Insert them into the incisions.

9 Cut the two red grapes in half lengthwise. Cut one half in two.

10 Place the two halves against the body to make legs and boots.

11 Cut the top and bottom from the other green apple. Make an incision ½ in. deep around the apple to mark the brim of the hat.

12 Slice off the top of the hat. Carve the sides as shown, leaving a brim on at the bottom.

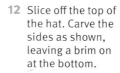

13 Cut the top off the red apple. Then cut a thick slice for the collar.

14 Lay the collar on the body. Place the head and hat on top.

15 You can also leave the skin on the top (step 12). Use the ground cherry as a pompom.

Ladybug

INGREDIENTS

1 red apple
1 slice of green apple
6 blue grapes
2 red grapes

1 Cut off the top of the red apple on an oblique angle.

2 This is the base.

3 Cut a thin round slice from the rest of the apple. This is the body.

4 Place the base skin side down.

5 Cut six narrow segments from around the edge of the slice of green apple.

6 Cut out legs of peel. Place these on the base. Place the body over top.

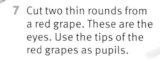

7 Cut two thin rounds from a red grape. These are the eyes. Use the tips of the red grapes as pupils.

8 Cut two large round slices from the red apple as shown. These are the wings.

9 Cut six tiny tips from the blue grapes. These are the spots.

10 Place the spots on the wings. Lay the wings on the body. Add the eyes.

Monkey

INGREDIENTS
2 red apples
1 slice of green apple
1 green grape
1 red grape

1 Cut an oblique slice from the top of a red apple. This is the lower lip.

2 Then cut another thin round slice. This is the upper lip.

3 Cut two rounds from the sides of the apple as shown. These are the ears.

4 The remainder of the apple is the head. Cut out two thin triangular sections from behind the two rounds. These are the eyebrows.

5 Insert the ears into the grooves.

6 Set the upper lip on the lower lip. Place the head on top of the lips.

7 Cut two oval slices from the green grape. Lay them on the cut rounds of the apple. These are the eyes.

8 Cut the tips off the red grapes. These are the pupils.

9 Place the eyebrows (step 4) above the eyes.

10 Cut a round slice from a green apple.

11 Cut off a small section. This is the nose.

12 Cut out nostrils as shown.

13 Lay the nose on the lips. For the body, cut a small round slice from other apple.

14 Place the body against the head. Cut out thin strips of peel for the arms, legs and tail.

15 You can also give the monkey a banana to hold.

Turtle

INGREDIENTS

1 yellow apple
1 red grape
1 green grape

1 Stand the apple on its top. Cut off a slice at an angle.

2 Lay the apple, skin side up. Cut a thin slice from the top.

3 Cut the slice into two parts as shown. It is the head.

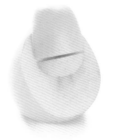

4 The remaining part of the apple is the body.

5 Lay the head on the body.

6 Cut two circles from a red grape. These are eyes.

7 Put the eyes on the head.

8 Put the seeds on the eyes. These are pupils.

9 Cut a green grape in half lengthwise.

10 Cut each half in half again. These are legs.

11 Put the legs on the body as shown.

Dragon

INGREDIENTS

2 green apples
1 red apple
1 side slice of yellow
    apple
1 green grape
2 red grapes

1 Core the green apple.

2 Cut a slice from one side. The remaining part of the apple is the body.

3 On the other side, cut the slot for the neck at the top of the apple.

4 Lay the body cut side down. Cut a narrow segment from each side of the neck slot.

5 Cut a round slice from the body, opposite to the neck side.

6 Cover the end with a side slice of the yellow apple.

7 Make a tail out of a side slice from the other green apple.

8 Cut teeth out on each side of the tail as shown.

9 Insert the tail into the hole in the body (step 5).

10 Cut two round thin side slices from the red apple. Carve the wings.

11 Cut a thin round slice of red apple in half. Shape each half into legs and feet.

12 Insert the wings into the slots. Place the legs under the body.

13 Cut a thin side slice and another slice from the green apple. Stack them as shown. This is the head.

14 The other half slice of red apple (step 11) is the neck. Cut out a slot to insert the head. Insert the neck in the body.

16 Cut a tongue out of red apple peel.

15 Cut two thin rounds from the green grape for the eyes. Use the tips of a red grape for the pupils.

Parrot

INGREDIENTS

2 green apples
1 red apple
1 yellow apple
1 green grape
2 red grapes

1 Core the green apple. Cut two round slices. The remaining part of the apple is the head.

2 Cut a vertical slot between the sliced areas to insert the beak.

3 Cut a thin round slice from the bottom of the apple.

4 Cut a side slice off the red apple. Cut it in half and join together as shown.

5 Carve the ends of the joined halves so that they fit in the beak slot. This is the top part of the beak.

6 Cut one more round slice off the red apple. Cut this in half and cut a small triangular section out of each half.

7 Place the two halves together. This is the lower part of the beak.

8 Insert it in the slot as shown.

9 Insert the top part of the beak.

10 Make two eyes with thin rounds of green grape and tips of red grape.

11 Cut legs out of a red apple slice as shown.

12 Cut the bottom off the other green apple. Cover with the yellow apple bottom slice. This is the body. Place the legs as shown.

13 Cut a round slice of green apple in half. This is the tail. Cut two side slices of yellow apple and place at the sides as wings.

14 Place the head on the body.

15 Cut out a crest from a slice of red apple.

16 Insert the crest into the core hole.

Flower

INGREDIENTS
1 green apple
1 red apple

1 Cut out five petals from around the top of the red apple.

2 Cut out the pulp from under each petal.

3 Carve petal contours around the center of the apple.

4 Cut this top part from the apple in a thick slice.

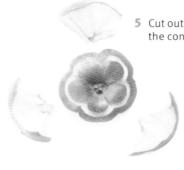

5 Cut out pulp from under the contoured area.

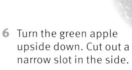

6 Turn the green apple upside down. Cut out a narrow slot in the side.

7 Cut out the first vein.

8 Cut out five more veins symmetrically.

9 Cut contours of the leaf.

10 Cut out points around the edge of the leaf.

11 Repeat steps 6–10 to cut four more leaves. Cut out contours under the leaves.

12 Cut out skin and pulp from around the leaves as shown.

13 Place the red flower on top.

Vase

INGREDIENTS

1 yellow apple
1 red currant stem

1 Cut a petal contour near the top of the apple.

2 Cut out a strip of the pulp from under the petal by holding the knife at a downward angle.

3 Repeat for five more petals.

4 Cut out a triangular piece between each petal, making a hollow tip.

5 Carve out and contour a raised "V" below the hollow tip.

6 Carve out a second raised "V" below the previous one.

7 Repeat between the rest of the petals.

8 Using a sharp, thin knife cut into the center of the apple at the edges of the petal designs.

9 Carefully separate the top from the base.

10 Core the base.

11 Hollow out the base, making a vase.

12 Make toothed incisions under the edge.

13 Cut out grooves as shown in the photo.

14 Lay the red currant stem in the vase.

15 Insert a toothpick for fastening the lid.

16 Spear the lid onto the toothpick.

Heart Apple

INGREDIENTS
1 red apple

1 Place the apple upside down. Cut out a heart, pointing the knife to the top center.

2 Cut a contour around the heart.

3 Cut out a strip of pulp from the contour, again at an angle.

4 Repeat for another heart larger than the first, as shown.

5 Cut out teeth along the external edge of the heart, as shown.

6 Cut out a heart on the lower side of the apple.

7 Cut out a contour around it. Cut out a strip of pulp from under it.

8 Cut out an arc near the heart.

9 Cut out teeth along the external edge of the arc.

10 Place the cut out hearts on top of the apple.

Star Apple

INGREDIENTS

1 green apple
1 red apple (optional)

1 Make a narrow cut across the bottom of the apple, holding a knife at a downward angle toward the center of the apple.

2 Make a symmetrical cut opposite, also angled toward the center. Remove the cut sections.

3 Cut out two more sections perpendicular to these.

4 Cut out four more sections to create a star.

5 Cut out a vertical section from the side of the apple.

6 Cut out a similar horizontal section across the middle of the vertical cut. These are the rays.

7 Cut out two more rays in between the existing ones to make a star.

8 Cut out the same stars all over the apple.

9 The cut-out sections can be inserted into the cut sections of the rays.

10 You can also cut sections from a red apple for added contrast.

Pineapple

INGREDIENTS

1 green apple
1 yellow apple

1 Make triangular cuts around the top of the yellow apple.

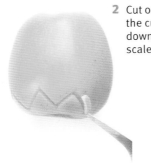

2 Cut out a strip of pulp from under the cut, holding the knife at a downward angle. These are the scales.

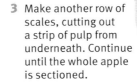

3 Make another row of scales, cutting out a strip of pulp from underneath. Continue until the whole apple is sectioned.

4 Make a triangular cut in the center of each scale and, lift the skin slightly so it extends out.

5 Core the apple.

6 Cut a large slice from the green apple.

7 Cut leaf contours with the tip of the knife.

8 Cut out the pieces, as shown.

9 Contour the underside of the interior leaves.

10 Insert the leaves into the top of the pineapple.

A FIREFLY BOOK

Published by Firefly Books Ltd. 2016

Copyright © 2016 Good Mood Editions Gmbh
Text copyright © 2016 Iryna Stepanova, Sergiy Kabachenko
Images copyright© 2016 Iryna Stepanova, Sergiy Kabachenko

First printing

PUBLISHER CATALOGING-IN-PUBLICATION DATA (U.S.)
Names: Stepanova, Iryna, author. | Kabachenko, Sergiy, author.
Title: Apple creatures : make your own / Iryna Stepanova, Sergiy Kabachenko.
Description: Richmond Hill, Ontario, Canada : Firefly Books, 2016. | Series: Make Your Own | Summary: Food presentation skills for cooks, chefs, and parents are provided with step by step instructions and photographs of each step.
Identifiers: ISBN 978-1-77085-853-4 (hardcover)
Subjects: LCSH: Cooking (Apples). | Food presentation. | Garnishes (Cooking).
Classification: LCC TX740.5S747 |DDC 641.819 – dc23

LIBRARY AND ARCHIVES CANADA CATALOGUING IN PUBLICATION
Stepanova, Iryna, author
Apple creatures : make your own / Iryna Stepanova and
Sergiy Kabachenko.
ISBN 978-1-77085-853-4 (hardback)
1. Food craft. 2. Food presentation. 3. Cooking (Garnishes).
4. Cooking (Apples). I. Kabachenko, Sergiy, author II. Title.
TX740.5.S73 2016   745.5   C2016-903712-6

Published in the United States by
Firefly Books (U.S.) Inc.
P.O. Box 1338, Ellicott Station
Buffalo, New York 14205

Published in Canada by
Firefly Books Ltd.
50 Staples Avenue, Unit 1
Richmond Hill, Ontario L4B 0A7

Cover and interior design: Peter Ross / Counterpunch Inc.

Printed in China

The publisher gratefully acknowledges the financial support for our publishing program by the Government of Canada through the Canada Book Fund as administered by the Department of Canadian Heritage.